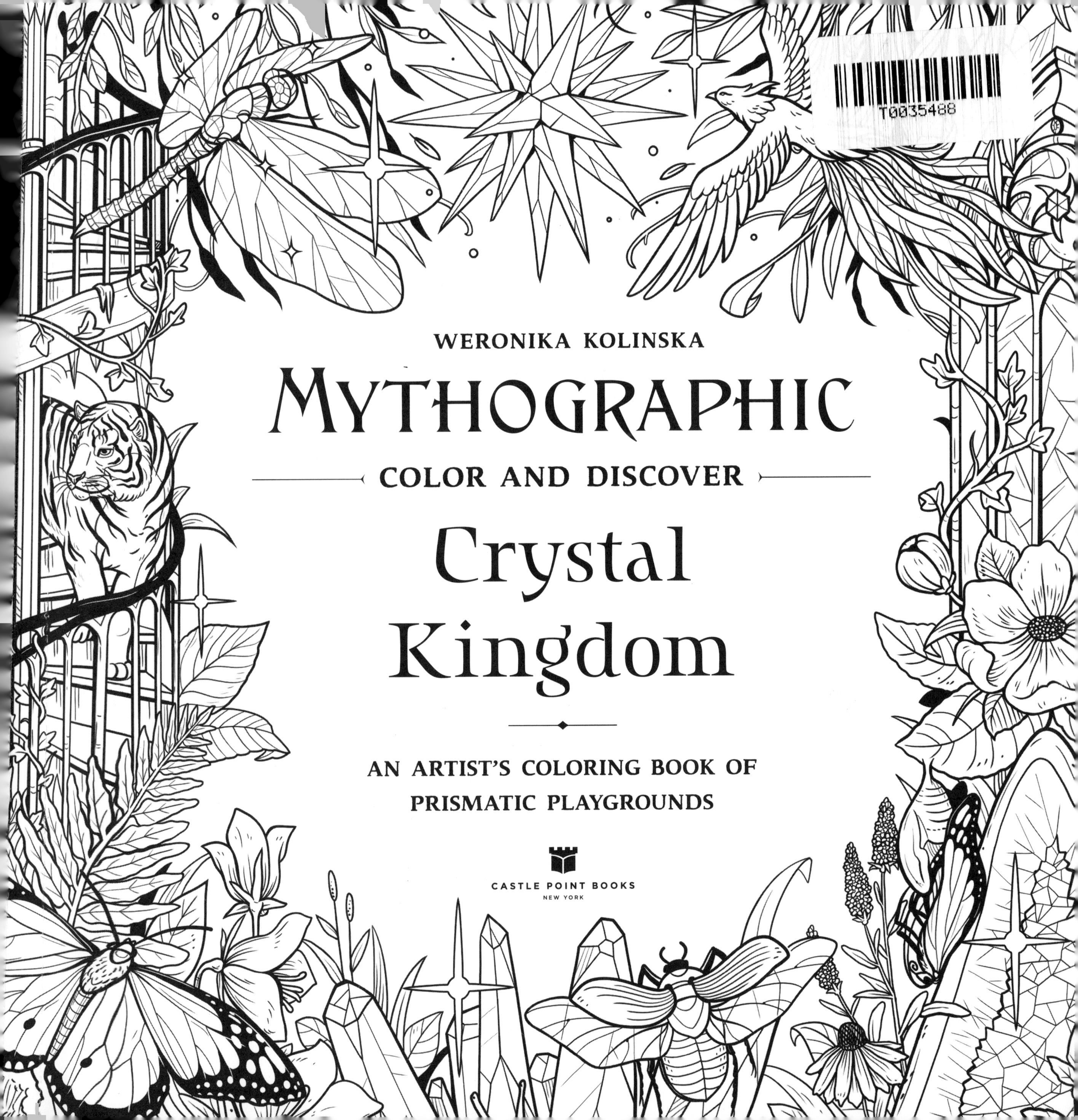

WERONIKA KOLINSKA

# MYTHOGRAPHIC

COLOR AND DISCOVER

# Crystal Kingdom

AN ARTIST'S COLORING BOOK OF PRISMATIC PLAYGROUNDS

CASTLE POINT BOOKS
NEW YORK

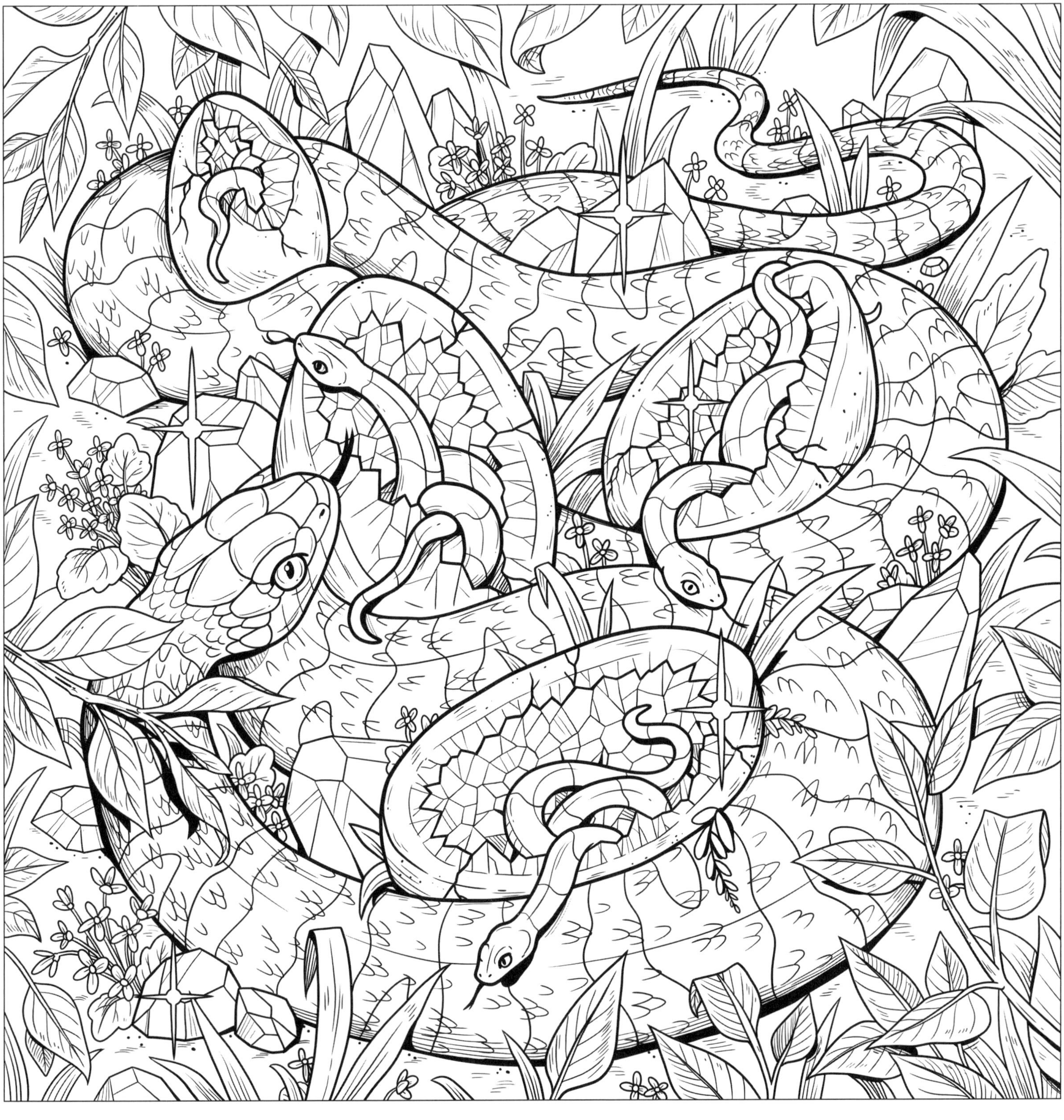

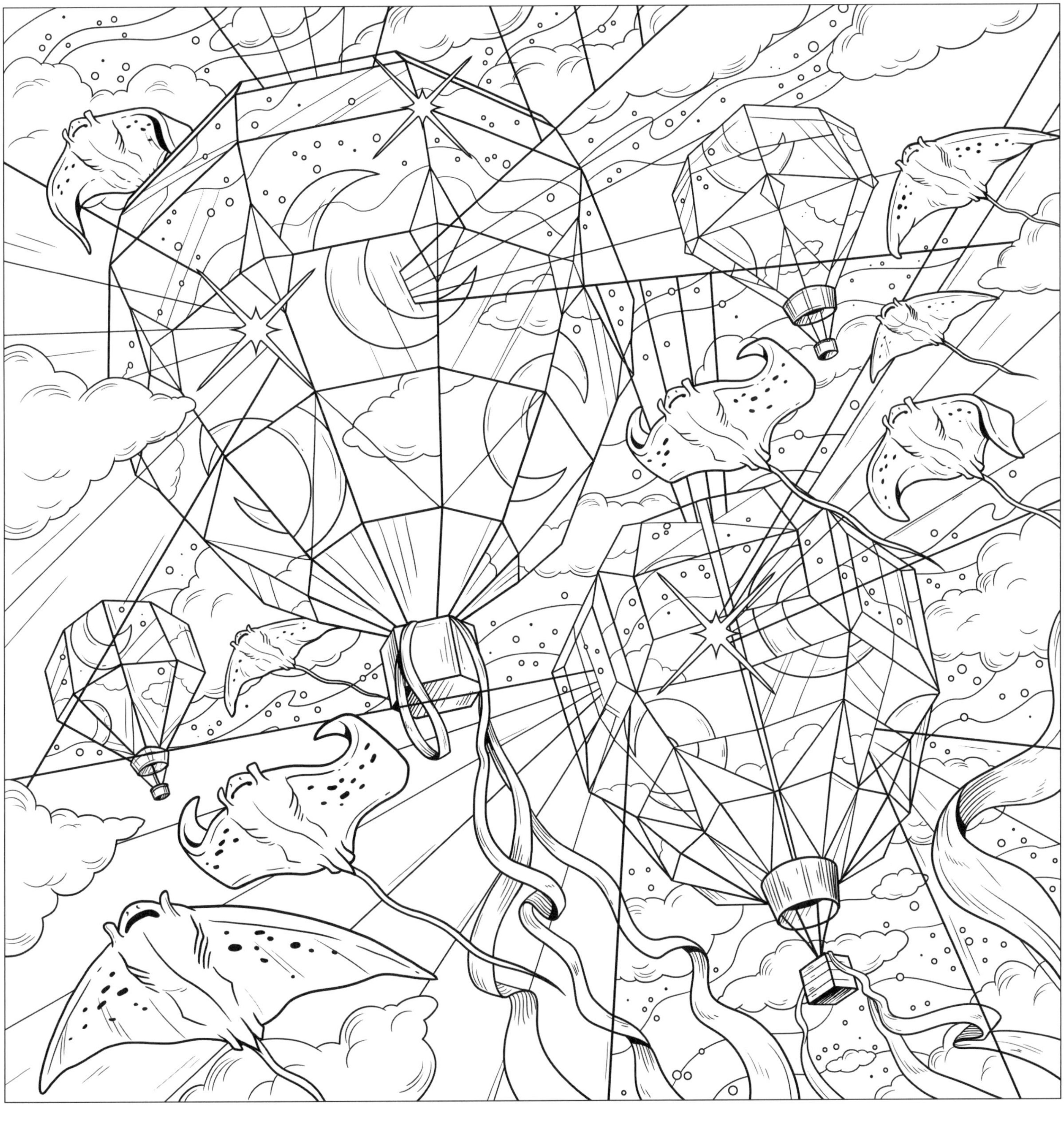

## Discover more of Mythographic

MYTHOGRAPHIC COLOR AND DISCOVER: CRYSTAL KINGDOM.

For information, address
St. Martin's Publishing Group, 120 Broadway, New York, NY 10271.

www.castlepointbooks.com

The Castle Point Books trademark is owned by Castle Point Publishing, LLC.
Castle Point books are published and distributed by St. Martin's Publishing Group.

ISBN 978-1-250-32426-9 (trade paperback)

Cover design by Young Lim
Edited by Monica Sweeney



First Edition: 2024

10 9 8 7 6 5 4 3 2 1